Go Free or Die

Go Free or Die

A Story about Harriet Tubman

by Jeri Ferris

illustrations by Karen Ritz

Macmillan/McGraw-Hill School Publishing Company
New York • Chicago • Columbus

For my mother, Eleanor
Free at last

For information regarding permission, write to Carolrhoda Books, Inc.,
241 First Avenue North, Minneapolis, MN 55401.

This edition is reprinted by special arrangement with Carolrhoda Books,
Inc., Minneapolis, MN. All rights reserved.

Macmillan/McGraw-Hill School Division
10 Union Square East
New York, New York 10003

Printed in the United States of America

ISBN 0-02-146223-2

5 6 7 8 9 MAZ 99 98 97 96

Table of Contents

AUTHOR'S NOTE

Harriet Tubman was born in 1820 on a plantation in Maryland. She and the rest of her family were slaves, and their master, Edward Brodas, could work them or sell them as he pleased. But Harriet was different from most slaves—she wondered why such things should be. Harriet believed that she had a right to go free or die. This is the story of her struggle for freedom for herself and for her people.

Chapter One

It was the middle of the morning. Harriet was walking home across the tobacco fields when she saw her mother, Rit, running after Mr. Brodas. "Master," cried Rit as she ran, "please, Master, she's only six years old!"

Harriet began to tremble with fear, and her bare feet felt cold on the warm dirt. The empty water buckets she was carrying suddenly seemed as heavy as stones.

The dark brown horse stopped in front of Harriet. She looked up past the horse's rolling eyes to Mr. Brodas, who was towering over her. "Girl," Mr. Brodas said briskly, "I'm sending you off to work for another farmer. Follow me, quickly now."

"No!" Harriet cried, seeing the frightened look on her mother's face. "I don't want to go away!"

Mr. Brodas sighed impatiently and tapped Harriet with his riding whip. But Harriet couldn't move. She felt as if she'd been planted in the dirt. Mr. Brodas raised his whip again.

Suddenly Harriet dropped the buckets and ran into her mother's arms. Rit held her daughter tight as the whip came down on her own back. "Out of the way, Rit," said Mr. Brodas. Leaning down from his horse, he pulled Harriet away from her mother and carried her over to a woman seated in a wagon at the side of the road.

"Please, Master," Rit begged as Mr. Brodas put Harriet on the wagon, "don't take Harriet. She's the third baby you've taken from me."

But Mr. Brodas had decided to rent Harriet out to a farmer's wife who was looking for a young slave girl. Brodas watched all the slave children as they grew. He noticed that Harriet carried water to the hot, thirsty slaves working in the fields. He saw that she helped her mother and father, who came home exhausted every night, long after dark. So when Mrs. Cook came to rent a good worker, Mr. Brodas chose Harriet.

As the wagon started off, Harriet could hardly see the dusty road through her tears. Behind her she heard her mother calling, "Be strong, child, and the good Lord will help you!"

The wagon rattled on, taking Harriet farther and farther away from home. Would she ever see her family again? Harriet bit her lip and stared straight ahead, trying to be strong. But the tears wouldn't stop. Finally she covered her face with her hands and sobbed. The next second she felt a harsh blow on the back of her neck and heard her new mistress scold, "Stop that crying, girl! Now sit up and be quiet."

"Yes, Missus," Harriet whispered. Tears still trickled down her face, but she didn't make a sound.

The sun had set by the time they came to the farm where Harriet was to work. She followed her mistress into the cooking shed next to the house.

"Here's your supper," said Mrs. Cook. She handed Harriet a piece of corn bread from a pan next to the fireplace. "That's where you sleep, over there by the fire." She frowned at Harriet.

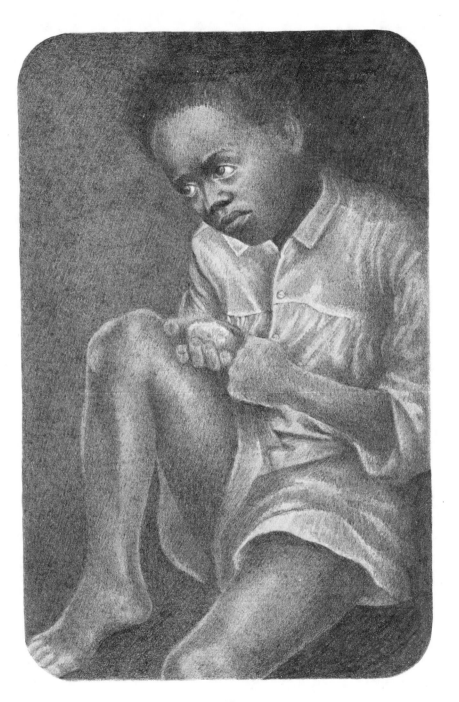

13

"There'll be no laziness here. Be ready to work first thing in the morning."

Mrs. Cook turned and went out, leaving Harriet alone in the small, dark shed. Harriet looked down at the corn bread in her hand. She couldn't eat. She curled up in the smoky corner, with only her thin shirt for a blanket, and she cried herself to sleep.

Early the next morning, Harriet began to work for Mrs. Cook. She was to help her mistress make cloth. "Here's where you stand, Harriet, and here is the yarn." Mrs. Cook spoke in a cross voice. "Now you pull carefully and wind the yarn like this."

Harriet watched her mistress and tried to wind the yarn just right. "Like this, Missus?"

"Carefully, or you'll break it! Do this right or I'll take the whip to you! Now you stand there and keep working." Harriet stood for hours and hours, winding the yarn and sneezing from the dust in the air.

Every day she worked in the dusty room and every night she slept close to the fire to keep warm. She often dreamed that she was back home, outside in the fresh, clean air, running through the woods while Daddy Ben cut down trees for Mr. Brodas. But her mistress kept her inside, day after day, cleaning and winding the yarn and choking on the fuzzy dust.

Then Harriet came down with the measles. Mrs. Cook sent her straight back to Mr. Brodas, and Mr. Brodas took her to her parents' cabin.

That night Mama Rit hugged her daughter tight and rocked her gently while Daddy Ben smoothed Harriet's ragged blanket out on the dirt floor, where all the children slept.

It was dark inside the windowless log cabin. The only light came from a large fireplace, which took up most of one wall. Harriet slowly looked around the cabin, thinking how happy she was to be back home. The battered chairs leaned crookedly against the wall. The two iron pots hung by the fire. Yes, it's still the same, Harriet thought as she fell asleep.

In the morning Harriet's family was up and at work before the sun rose. Harriet stayed in the cabin alone by the fire, and Rit slipped away from her work at the Master's Big House as often as she could to care for her little girl.

When Harriet was well enough to leave the cabin, she found a sunny place outside to sit and watch the other children as they ran and played.

Her back itched under her scratchy shirt, but the soft, warm dust felt good to her bare toes. Out beyond the slave quarters, Harriet could see fields stretching away into the distance. Somewhere out there Daddy Ben was working. Somewhere farther she knew there was a lazy river winding its way through the woods.

Harriet laughed out loud with happiness. "Oh, Lord," she said, "thank you for bringing me home."

Harriet's master let her stay with her mother and father for a little while. Then, when she was seven, he rented her out again. Mama Rit cried but could do nothing.

Harriet and her parents stood outside their cabin as her new master drove up. Harriet held tightly to Daddy Ben's hand. "I remember our other little girls," Daddy Ben said quietly. "They were carrying water out to the fields, just trying to help, and Master put them in a slave gang going South." Daddy Ben bent down to hug Harriet. "Just took our two little ones. We couldn't even say good-bye."

Then it was time for Harriet to go. As the wagon jolted and bumped down the road, Harriet looked back at her mother and father standing together by the cabin. Again she wondered if this was the last time she would ever see them.

This time Harriet was put to work in a large plantation house. She scrubbed and dusted and cleaned. She worked all day long without time to rest or play. And the nights were worse. At night she had to look after the mistress's new baby.

"I don't ever want to hear the baby cry," said her mistress, Miss Susan. "You see this whip? You'll feel it if you let that baby wake up and cry."

Harriet struggled to keep her eyes open while she rocked the cradle all night, every night. Sometimes Harriet fell asleep and the baby cried. Then Harriet was whipped. Sometimes she didn't clean the house well enough to please Miss Susan. Then she was whipped again. Harriet's back and neck and legs were always sore from the stinging rawhide.

"Missus, I'm doing the best I can," Harriet cried. "Please, Missus, don't whip me." But Miss Susan didn't care that Harriet was only a little girl.

One day Harriet couldn't stand the whippings anymore, and she ran away. She ran as far as she could, and when she saw a large pigpen, she crawled under the fence and huddled in the corner. A huge mother pig with eight baby pigs glared at her, but Harriet was too tired to be frightened. She stayed with the pigs for a few days and ate the scraps of food they left in the mud. But at last she became so hungry that she had to go back to her mistress.

"You lazy, no-good nigger!" screamed Miss Susan as she got out the whip. "You're not worth the money I'm paying for you!"

She took Harriet back to Mr. Brodas. "This girl will never be any good as a house slave," Miss Susan told him angrily. "You should make her work in the fields."

Harriet was overjoyed to be out of Miss Susan's house, but her mother was worried. "Child," she said, stirring a pot of cornmeal mush over the fire, "don't you know you have to please those folks? They can do anything they want with you. You'd be better off working in the master's Big House than out in the fields. It takes a strong man to do fieldwork, Harriet, and you're just a little girl."

But Harriet's master did send her out to the fields. She learned how to plow the ground, hoe the weeds, chop the wood, load the wagons, and take care of the mules. She also learned to obey the overseer, the man who made sure the slaves did not stop working. He had a long, terrible whip that cut into the back of any slave who didn't work fast enough, so Harriet tried to work as fast as the grown-up slaves.

Chapter Two

Every day Harriet worked from the time the sun came up until it had set. She worked in the scorching heat and in the cold rain. Harriet was small and young, but she grew strong as she plowed and hoed and chopped.

Now that she was a field hand, she was given a long skirt to wear instead of just a child's shirt. When the skirt got in her way, she tucked it up over a rope tied around her waist. She still had no shoes, but her feet became tough and hard in the rocky soil of the fields.

The other field hands liked to listen to Harriet sing. "Harriet," they would call as they worked, "sing that song about Moses again." And Harriet would sing in her low voice the song the slaves loved best.

Go down, Moses,
Way down in Egypt land.
Tell old Pharaoh
Let my people go...

Sometimes, when the overseer wasn't looking, Harriet would lean on her hoe and watch the clouds drifting slowly overhead and the birds flying free in the sky. She wondered what it would be like to be free. She wondered how it would feel to walk down the road anywhere she wanted to go, to walk and talk and work and eat with no one standing over her with a whip. But when she asked the other slaves about it, they just shook their heads. They didn't know either.

In 1831 Harriet was 11 years old. She had been a field hand for four years, and she was almost as strong as a man. She began to wear a bandanna of bright-colored cloth around her head. This was a sign to everyone who saw her that she was growing up. Harriet was becoming a young woman.

That same year the slaves began to talk about a slave named Nat Turner. The talk spread in whispers from plantation to plantation. Nat Turner thought that slaves should kill their masters and escape to freedom. But most slaves refused to do such a terrible thing, no matter how cruel their masters were.

Even though Nat Turner's plan didn't work and he was captured, many slave owners were worried that their slaves might have the same idea. They were so afraid that they wouldn't let their slaves meet anymore. They wouldn't even let them sing their favorite song, the one about Moses. Harriet sang it anyway. As she sang she thought about Nat Turner. "There must be a better way to get freedom, Mama," she said one day. "And I'm going to find it."

Not long after Nat Turner was captured, Harriet heard about an underground road. She heard the other slaves whisper as they worked in the fields and as they rested in their cabins after dark. They talked about slaves who had disappeared. "Gone North on a secret road, the underground road," they whispered. "Gone North where everybody's free."

"An underground road?" asked Harriet. "A road that goes under the ground? Do you walk under the ground and come up into freedom?" But no one could tell her. No one had ever come back from that underground road.

One afternoon, when Harriet had just turned 13, she saw a slave try to escape. Harriet was working in the cornfield with the other field hands when she saw Jim, a strong, young slave, glance at the overseer. The next minute Jim was running as fast as he could across the field. The overseer, who was on horseback, galloped after Jim, shouting and waving his whip. Harriet threw down the corn she was holding and ran after both of them. She wanted to see if Jim would escape on the underground road.

She saw Jim run inside a little store at the crossroad with the overseer at his heels. As Harriet ran up to the door, the overseer dragged Jim out from behind the counter and shouted at Harriet. "You, girl! Hold that boy, and don't let him get away!"

The overseer shook out his whip, expecting Harriet to hold on to the runaway slave while he was being punished. But Harriet did not move. Jim just wanted to be free, the same as she did.

At that moment she knew she couldn't act like a slave anymore. She *could not* do what the overseer ordered.

Jim dashed past Harriet and out the door. The furious overseer picked up a heavy lead weight and threw it as hard as he could after the runaway, but the weight missed Jim and hit Harriet instead. She fell to the ground and lay still.

Harriet was carried back to the slave quarters, bleeding from a long open wound on her forehead. Her eyes were closed. As her parents looked at her lying on the dirt floor, they thought she would surely die. Once again Rit nursed her daughter.

Mr. Brodas came down to see Harriet and shook his head. She was no good to him anymore. He tried to sell her several times, but no one else wanted the half-conscious slave either. All of the slaves talked about Harriet. If she ever got better, they said, the master would sell her South. Master didn't keep dangerous slaves who did not obey the overseer.

The corn picking was over. Harvest season passed. Christmas came and went. Harriet's family washed her and fed her and watched over her, but still she lay on the floor of the cabin without moving. Then their prayers were answered. Very slowly Harriet began to get better. "Mama," she called weakly one night. "Mama, am I home?"

"Thank the Lord," Rit cried. "He's brought you through the valley!" In the light of the fire, Harriet could see tears on her mother's face.

Harriet got stronger. She could sit up and eat and stand, but her head always hurt. Worst of all, at any time she might suddenly fall down, sound asleep. She would fall asleep in the middle of a sentence or while she was eating or walking or working. She never knew when this would happen, and there was nothing she could do to stop it.

Harriet remembered why she had not obeyed the overseer. She was not going to act like a slave anymore. She couldn't live the way the other slaves did. They always smiled at the master and tried to stay away from his whip. They never knew when he might sell them or their children. Harriet began to think harder about how she could go free.

As soon as she was strong again, Harriet heard that she and her brothers were going to be sold South. It was just as the other slaves had said. She would be chained with her brothers in a gang of slaves for the long walk to the Deep South. I'll never be free now, Harriet thought. She remembered the clank of the chains on her two sisters, years ago, as they were dragged down the road, screaming and crying, and she was afraid.

But before Harriet was sold, Mr. Brodas died.

John Stewart, the new master, rode down to the slave quarters to see his property. He looked Harriet over carefully.

"Girl," Mr. Stewart said at last, "you look plenty strong to me. I want you to work outside. You can help Ben cut down trees. Get going now!" Mr. Stewart gave Harriet a tap with the end of his short whip and rode off.

"Thank you, Lord," Harriet whispered as she ran out to find Daddy Ben.

Harriet was now 14 years old. She was short, only five feet tall, and her face was plain. Below her colorful bandanna, a scar stood out on her forehead. Her dark eyes were bright, and her mouth was set and determined. Even though she might have a sleeping spell in the middle of a job, she could do as much work as any man.

Day after day Harriet and her father worked in the woods, filling wagons with logs for Mr. Stewart to sell at the Baltimore shipyards. As they worked, Daddy Ben watched Harriet. He saw that she turned away or stood in stubborn silence when Master Stewart rode by.

One day he asked her why she didn't smile at the master and try to please him. Harriet set down her ax. "Daddy Ben," she said slowly, "please don't worry—but I can't be a slave all my life. I've got to go free!"

Daddy Ben sighed. "Take care, child," he warned. "The master won't let you go."

From that day on, Ben did not ask Harriet what she was thinking. But he began to teach her all he knew about the woods and swamps and rivers of Maryland. Harriet learned which plants and berries could be eaten and which could be used as medicine. She learned how to go north at night by watching the North Star. She learned how to catch fish and rabbits. She learned how to move silently through the woods, as silently as a moth.

Every night Harriet stood outside the cabin looking at the North Star. When she slept she dreamed about going free, but when she woke up she worried that if she tried to escape, she would have a sleeping spell while she was hiding from the slave catchers. She knew that would be the end of her freedom.

Once Rit heard Harriet talking in her sleep about being free. She shook Harriet angrily. "Hush, child! Don't you be talking like that. You'll get yourself sold South yet, and then what will I do?"

"Mama, don't worry," Harriet said softly. "But there are two things I have a right to. Either freedom or death. If I can't have one, then I will have the other, because no one is going to catch me alive." Harriet laughed and hugged her mother so Rit wouldn't be afraid. "Anyway, I'm not going anywhere just now."

Chapter Three

For 15 more years, Harriet worked as a slave. She plowed fields and drove mules. She chopped down trees and loaded wagons with logs for the shipyards. She would not smile and act like a slave, but she worked so hard that Mr. Stewart didn't sell her. In fact he even let her hire herself out to other farmers, as long as she gave him part of the money she earned.

During this time, when Harriet was about 24, Mr. Stewart gave her permission to marry John Tubman, a free black man. John had been given his freedom by his former master and could keep all the money he earned, when he could find a job. But it was hard for a free black man to find work in a slave state, so John was happy to have a hardworking wife who brought a little money home.

Even though her husband was free, Harriet was still a slave. John did not want to hear about

Harriet's dream for freedom. He was happy living in Harriet's cabin in the slave quarters.

So Harriet kept her dream hidden in her heart. But every day as she worked, she told herself, "Somehow I must take my freedom, because surely no one is going to give it to me." Still she waited. She did not want to leave her husband or her mother and father. And she never knew when she might fall down asleep.

Then early one morning, as she drove the mules and wagon to the woods, Harriet saw a woman waiting for her in a plain, black buggy. The woman softly called out Harriet's name. Harriet knew from the woman's simple, dark dress and bonnet that she was a Quaker. She also knew that Quakers believed slavery was wrong and that she could trust this woman.

As Harriet came close to the buggy, she felt warmed by the woman's smile. "How do you know me, Missus?" Harriet asked, looking around quickly to make sure no one saw them.

"I know you by the scar on your forehead," said the woman. "I came to find you today because we Quakers have heard that Mr. Stewart needs money. He is planning to sell you for a good price to a cotton plantation in the South."

Harriet's heart jumped with fear at these words, but she listened quietly as the woman went on.

"We try to help slaves who want to be free," the woman said, and then she told Harriet about the underground road. "It isn't a real road, but it is a way to freedom in the North, where slavery is illegal. We call this road the Underground Railroad. The railroad stations are the houses of people who help runaway slaves, and at each station there is a conductor who helps to show the way."

"Oh, Missus," said Harriet, "how do I find this railroad?" The Quaker woman leaned out of her buggy and whispered to Harriet. Then she handed her a small piece of paper and quickly drove off.

Holding the paper tightly in her hand, Harriet watched until the horse and buggy were gone. Because slaves were not allowed to go to school, Harriet could not read the writing on the paper, but she knew it was a message that would help her go free. "Give this paper to the first conductor on the Underground Railroad," the Quaker woman had said.

Harriet closed her eyes and took deep breaths of air to quiet her pounding heart. This is the time, she thought. Now is the time to take my freedom. She led the mules on into the woods, trying to act as she always did, in case someone was watching.

Later that day a slave boy slipped away from the Big House to find Harriet. He whispered to her that Mr. Stewart had already sold her to a slave gang going to the Deep South. The overseer of the slave gang was to take her in the morning.

As the boy ran quickly back to the Big House, Harriet stood alone by the wagon she was loading. "Lord," she said, "you know my troubles. I might fall asleep while I'm trying to find the road. But I can't go South. I've got to go free!"

Harriet believed God had sent the Quaker woman to show her the way to freedom, and she believed she was ready. She thought sadly about John and the rest of her family. Somehow she would come back for them, she promised herself. She would lead them all to freedom.

That night after John was asleep, Harriet tied a little cloth bag to the rope around her waist. In the bag she put some corn bread and salt pork and the paper the Quaker woman had given her. She silently slipped out of the cabin, ran across an open field, and disappeared into the woods. Harriet knew she had to be far, far away when the overseer came for her in the morning.

The night was clear and still, and the North Star led her toward freedom. Harriet repeated to herself what the Quaker woman had told her: "Follow the Choptank River 40 miles to its beginning. Then follow the road to Camden, and look for a white house with green shutters. A conductor will help you there."

All that night Harriet walked and ran toward the safest place to wade into the river, a place where it wasn't so deep. She wanted to sing for joy, but she stayed silent. The birds didn't even move from their nests as she passed. As she neared the Choptank River, the ground under her bare feet began to feel wet and muddy. The woodland was becoming swampy, with large pools of water shining in the moonlight.

Harriet thought about the slave catchers and the dogs that ran with their noses to the ground. They would be coming after her in the morning. She remembered what Daddy Ben had told her. "Those hunting dogs can't follow a person through the water, Harriet. Their sniffing doesn't work in the water."

She set her mouth tight and stepped into the swampy water. Her feet slipped in the mud and hanging branches hit her face, but she didn't stop.

"I've got to get to the river before I can stop to rest," she said to herself over and over.

As the sky lightened, the stars began to fade away. Before long Harriet could not see the North Star at all. She heard the birds singing as they woke up. Soon the sun would rise, strong and hot. Harriet knew the overseer was looking for her by now, and she shivered in the warm air.

"Am I going the right way? I have to go north, toward the river, but which way is north?" For a moment Harriet was frightened and looked wildly about. Then she remembered Daddy Ben's words. "When the North Star is gone, look for the soft, green moss growing on one side of the trees. That's the north side."

Harriet hurried through the prickly weeds, watching for the mossy side of the trees. Her feet and long skirt were covered with mud. Just as she thought she couldn't run anymore, she saw the Choptank River through the trees, sparkling in the morning sun. She walked to the edge of the woods and looked up and down the river. She was alone.

Harriet ate a piece of the corn bread from her bag and found fresh water to drink. Then she held on to a long branch and slid down the slippery riverbank into the muddy water. The dogs wouldn't find her tracks there.

Water swirled and bubbled around her as she waded along the edge of the river. Harriet's long skirt got heavier and heavier, but every time she thought of stopping, she seemed to hear dogs barking behind her.

All day long Harriet waded up the river. The leafy branches that bent over the riverbank shaded her from the hot sun, and by late afternoon she was nearing the place where the river began. (By this time Harriet had walked from Maryland into Delaware.) Little by little the river narrowed and the level of the water dropped. Soon Harriet was wading in a little stream that only came up to her ankles, and she could touch the bushes on both sides of the water.

Harriet kept walking until there was nothing left of the river except a trickle of water bubbling up out of the rocky ground. She stopped and listened. She heard the evening song of a bird coming from one of the trees that surrounded her, then all was still.

"Well, I've come to the beginning of the river," she sighed. "Thank you, Lord, for bringing me safe so far."

The sun was setting and Harriet was tired. This was her second night without any sleep. She felt cold in her damp, muddy dress, but she couldn't make a fire to warm herself. A fire could be seen by slave catchers. She hid in some tall weeds under an old tree and ate the rest of her corn bread and salt pork. Just enough time for a rest, she thought. Then I must find the first stop on the Underground Railroad.

When it was completely dark, Harriet stood up. She took a last drink of water and walked quickly to the edge of the woods. In the moonlight she could make out a rocky dirt road heading north. It was the road to Camden, just a few miles away. Harriet took a deep breath, looked up at the North Star, and stepped out of the woods. The night was quiet.

She began to run through the weeds by the side of the road, hoping that the slave catchers had stopped for the night. Then it happened. Without warning she fell down beside the road in a deep sleep.

She woke up to the sound of horses' hooves clattering on the rocky road. A group of men rode past Harriet as she huddled in the weeds. "Where could that girl be?" one of the men shouted angrily. "Do you think she got this far?" The horses stopped. Harriet was afraid to breathe.

"Let's go back," another man said. "There's no runaway slave on this road. We'll get the dogs and look again in the morning." Harriet heard the horses turn and gallop back down the road.

When the night was quiet again, Harriet slowly got up. She knew she had to get to Camden before morning.

As the first pink light of dawn began to touch the sky, Harriet came to the top of a hill and saw a small town below her. No one was up yet. No one saw her. Carefully Harriet crept closer, looking for a white house with green shutters. Then she saw it, a little white house all by itself at the edge of town. A black buggy stood outside. Harriet ran to the back of the house. She was shaking as she knocked on the door. What if she had made a mistake?

The door was opened by a tall woman, who swiftly pulled Harriet in and closed the door. Without speaking, Harriet took the paper from her bag and waited as the woman read it.

"Welcome, Harriet," the woman said in a warm voice. "I am Eliza Hunn. I am glad to see thee.

Thou must be terribly tired and hungry after such a long, hard walk." Mrs. Hunn put her arm around Harriet and led her into the kitchen. "Come in and have breakfast with us, Harriet. Then thou can rest."

For three days Harriet stayed with this gentle Quaker family. She ate with them and talked with them, and at night she slept in a soft bed for the first time in her life.

On the fourth day, Ezekiel Hunn said it was safe for Harriet to go on. Mrs. Hunn gave her fresh, clean clothes and a new bag of food for the next part of her journey. That evening as the sun set, Harriet and Mr. Hunn went out to the black buggy that stood in front of the house. As Mr. Hunn hitched up the horse, Harriet climbed in the buggy and hid under a blanket in the back.

Mr. Hunn gathered up the reins and they started off. The horse trotted briskly through the dark streets of Camden. No one seemed interested in the black buggy with its silent driver. When they came to the woods on the other side of Camden, Mr. Hunn stopped the buggy. The road was empty.

"Harriet," he said, helping her out of the buggy. "I am sorry I cannot take thee any farther, but it is not safe for thee here. Slave catchers are watching for runaways on the road up ahead." He pointed north, through the woods. "The next station is in Wilmington, a much bigger town than Camden. It is a long walk. It will take thee two nights, but thou will have woods to hide in all the way. Just before Wilmington, thou will come to a graveyard. Wait there for the next conductor." Mr. Hunn took Harriet's hand as he said good-bye. "God be with thee, Harriet."

Harriet thanked him with tears in her eyes. Then she turned and disappeared into the woods.

Chapter Four

Now she was alone again, with only the North Star to show her the way. It was a warm night. The gentle wind wrapped her in its soft breath. Harriet heard it whispering in the treetops as she walked silently through the woods. She walked north all night, and when morning came, she found a hiding place in the hollow of a tree. Harriet rested there, hidden from the slave catchers, until the sun went down.

As darkness crept through the woods on the second night, Harriet watched for the stars to appear in the sky before she started north again. "I'm getting close to freedom, Lord, I know I am," she said as she pushed through the bushes and clumps of grass.

Hours later Harriet came to a graveyard at the edge of the woods. She saw a man walking among the tombstones, and her heart almost stopped. Was he a ghost? Was he a slave catcher? Hiding in the tall weeds, she silently moved closer. The man was talking to himself. "I have the ticket for the railroad," he said. "I have the ticket for the railroad." Harriet stood up and walked toward him.

"Harriet?" he asked in a friendly voice. "I've been waiting for you. Hurry now, before it gets too light." He handed her a shovel and a pile of workman's clothes: a hat, heavy shoes, and overalls to go over her long dress.

"I'm Mr. Trent, Harriet. You're going to walk in to Wilmington as my workman. We'll pass guards watching the road for runaway slaves, but just follow me and don't say a word."

Soon Harriet was ready. Her bandanna and scar were hidden under the workman's hat. She put the shovel over her shoulder and walked behind Mr. Trent toward the bridge that led to Wilmington. Harriet saw groups of men standing by the road looking closely at every black person who passed. At the entrance to the bridge, guards waited on horseback. Harriet's heart pounded so hard she thought the slave catchers would hear it, but after one look, they paid no attention to Mr. Trent and his helper.

Harriet followed Mr. Trent into Wilmington. She had never seen such a busy, noisy town before.

The roads were filled with horses and buggies and people hurrying here and there. Big square buildings seemed to push in at her from both sides of the long streets. They walked on through the town until Mr. Trent stopped in front of a small shop. The owner of the shop, Thomas Garrett, was expecting Harriet.

As Mr. Trent said good-bye, he warned Harriet to take great care. "It's very dangerous here, Harriet, because this is the last town before you reach the free state of Pennsylvania. Slave catchers are watching to be sure no runaway slaves cross the line into Pennsylvania. But with God's help, you will soon be free!"

Harriet rested for a day in Mr. Garrett's home. Then on Sunday, she dressed in new clothes. "Many people want to see the slaves go free, Harriet," Mr. Garrett told her. "These people provide clothes for runaway slaves to wear."

Harriet put on a hat with a long veil that covered her face. Then Mr. Garrett helped her into his buggy. As their horse trotted through town, they looked as if they were just taking a Sunday drive. No one would know that the well-dressed lady in the buggy was really a runaway slave.

When they reached the wooded countryside

north of Wilmington, Mr. Garrett stopped the horse. "I must turn back here, Harriet. No one is watching just now, but be very careful. There are only a few miles to walk before thou will see a wooden sign at the crossroad. Look for this word." He gave her a paper with *Pennsylvania* printed on it. "That sign marks the line between the slave states of the South and the free states of the North. Then go straight down the road to Philadelphia, the first big town in Pennsylvania." Mr. Garrett smiled at Harriet. "God surely has sent a special angel of mercy to keep thee safe all this way. Thou art almost free!"

Mr. Garrett's buggy turned back toward Wilmington. Harriet stood for a minute, looking at the empty road in front of her. Soon she would be free! As she headed North, her feet seemed as light as angel's wings. On she ran, looking for the wooden sign.

Suddenly she felt afraid. It was too dangerous to be out on the road. She turned and ran into the woods. Moments later two horsemen galloped past, shouting and laughing. Then the road was quiet again, but Harriet stayed in the shadowy woods.

Harriet ran until she saw a crossroad ahead.

There was a small sign on a post by the side of the road. The letters on the sign were the same as the letters on the paper in her hand. Slowly she left the safety of the trees and walked until she could touch the warm wood of the little sign that marked her freedom. "Thank you, Lord," she whispered, kneeling on the ground. "You brought me safely here." Harriet wiped the tears from her face. She looked at her hands to see if she was still the same person, now that she was free.

At last Harriet got to her feet and stood in the middle of the road. "Oh, Lord, look! There's such a glory over everything. The sun looks like gold on the fields. I feel as if I'm in heaven!" Harriet sang and cried for joy as she walked down that free road toward Philadelphia.

"I'm free. I'm free at last!"

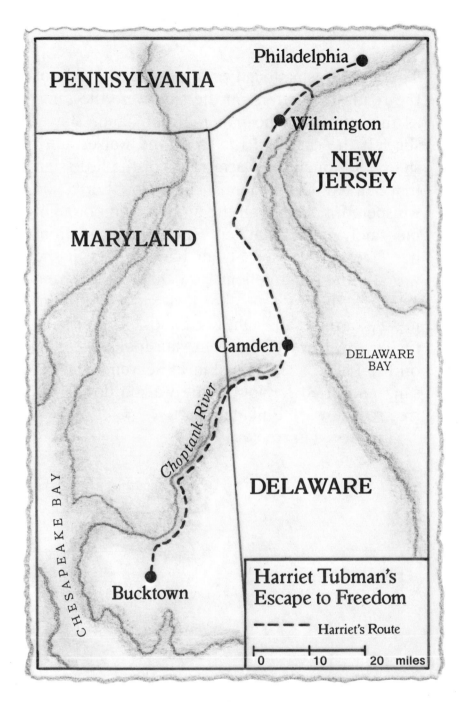

PENNSYLVANIA

Philadelphia

Wilmington

NEW
JERSEY

MARYLAND

Camden

DELAWARE
BAY

Choptank River

DELAWARE

CHESAPEAKE BAY

Bucktown

Harriet Tubman's
Escape to Freedom

- - - - Harriet's Route

0   10   20   miles

EPILOGUE

Harriet was free, but she did not forget her family or her people. Time after time she returned to the South, and time after time she walked back across the line of freedom, bringing others with her. Her friends in the North warned her that she would surely be caught if she kept going back, but Harriet was very careful.

She often disguised herself so the slave catchers would not recognize her if they saw her. On one trip back to her old home, Harriet even fooled her former master, John Stewart. As she neared Mr. Stewart's plantation, she bought two live chickens. She tied the chickens by their feet and let them dangle, squawking, from her waist.

Then she stooped over like an old woman and hobbled down the road. Suddenly, just as she had expected, she saw Mr. Stewart heading straight toward her. She let the chickens go.

Mr. Stewart saw a poor, old black woman, bent and lame and wearing a floppy sunbonnet, trying to catch two chickens that were fluttering away from her. He laughed, slapped his knee, and went on his way. When Harriet left his plantation and headed North again, some of Mr. Stewart's most valuable slaves went with her.

On each trip South, Harriet walked through woods and swampy river bottoms, always looking for safe hiding places to use when she came back that way. She hid in buggies and wagons driven by underground-railroad conductors, and she learned where slave catchers were waiting and watching. But things could go wrong at any moment.

If the conductor who was supposed to help her was suddenly put in jail, Harriet would quickly lead her exhausted group of escaped slaves another way. If a baby cried while they were hiding, Harriet would be ready with some sleeping medicine. If dogs were on their trail, Harriet would silently guide her group through icy, black swamp water until the dogs and the slave catchers gave up.

Slaves began to call Harriet "Moses," because, like Moses, she led her people out of captivity. When they heard that soft, low voice singing "Go down, Moses," outside their cabins, they knew she had come to set more people free.

Naturally the slave owners were furious. How could this black woman—a slave who still belonged to John Stewart, if he could ever lay hands on her—keep walking off with their property? They raised the reward for Harriet's capture to $40,000, a fortune in those days. Posters with Harriet's name and description were nailed to trees and buildings. Slave catchers lined the road to Wilmington, eager to collect the enormous reward. Meanwhile Harriet was making plans to rescue her own family.

Of course Harriet hadn't forgotten her husband, John Tubman, but she had learned that he'd forgotten her. John had married someone else. At first Harriet was terribly sad. Then she was terribly angry. Then, as she told a friend, she decided to drop him out of her heart.

Harriet was working as a scrubwoman in Philadelphia, to earn money for the supplies she would need for her next trip South, when she heard that her three brothers had been sold. They were to be sent to the Deep South the day after Christmas. Harriet immediately started out for Maryland, and one week later, on Christmas Eve, she slipped into a shed near the family cabin.

A small slave boy carried a message to her brothers, and after dark they came to the shed. Harriet wept with joy at seeing them again, but she was also sad because she could not let her mother know she was there. Old Rit would be so overcome with joy at seeing her daughter and so filled with grief that her boys were leaving, that others would surely hear and Harriet would be found.

So Harriet made a hard decision. None of her brothers or their families could go to the Christmas dinner Rit had prepared for the next day. They must stay away from their mother, lest their emotions give the plan away. Instead they would prepare for their escape.

Christmas was a sad, sad day. Through the cracks in the shed, Harriet watched her mother go to the door of the cabin again and again, looking for her boys. Harriet's brothers wept when they saw their mother's grief. "It's better for her that she not know, it's better that she not know," they said through gritted teeth.

But Harriet just had to tell Daddy Ben where

they were. She sent a message for him to come to the shed without telling Rit, and soon he was there. But when he entered the shed, his eyes were closed tight and his head was turned away. He hugged Harriet and touched her face and the scar on her forehead, without opening his eyes. He hugged his boys too, without looking at them.

"God keep you safe," Daddy Ben whispered. "I must truthfully tell Master that I have not seen you this day." Tears slid down his cheeks as he held his children tight. "God willing, we will meet again." Without once opening his eyes, he turned and left.

When it was dark, Harriet and her brothers and their families slipped into the woods and headed North. Back in the Master's Big House, the Christmas party was noisy with games and laughter. Back in their mother's little cabin, the Christmas meal lay cold and untouched.

After leading her brothers to freedom, Harriet was ready at last to bring out the most important slaves of all—Old Rit and Daddy Ben. It would be terribly difficult, because the two old people were in their seventies. They couldn't walk through the woods and swamps, and they certainly couldn't run.

What's more, Harriet had to get them safely all

the way to Canada. In 1850 a harsh new fugitive slave law had been passed. Any slave who had escaped to the free states in the North could be captured and taken back to the South if two white men swore that slave was escaped property. Slaves were not safe anywhere in the United States. They had to keep running until they got to Canada.

Harriet made her plans carefully, packed her cloth bag with food, and started South. As she had expected, her mother greeted her with tears and sobs of joy. But Harriet had not expected to find Daddy Ben in jail. He was accused of helping other slaves escape and had been put in an old one-room wooden jail until his trial.

Harriet solved the problem of Daddy Ben by finding a slave brave enough to saw through the rickety wall of the jail that very night. Then she sent a message to Mr. Jackson, an old friend who had helped her before, and together they worked out a plan. Mr. Jackson would gather the supplies that Harriet needed, and she would put them together. Mr. Jackson also had a horse. It was an old, broken-down horse, but it would do.

All afternoon Harriet worked in the shed. She stuffed a tattered shirt with straw and made a soft collar for the horse's neck. She made a harness out of a piece of rope and tied it to the collar. She took two tall, rusty buggy wheels and fastened a board between them. Then she hung a second board below the first board. On these boards, between these wheels, her parents would ride to freedom.

Soon after dark Daddy Ben crawled through the sawed-out hole in the wall of the jail and hurried home. Quickly Harriet helped her parents onto their new buggy. She climbed up beside them, picked up the reins, and drove slowly out to the road that would take them North. When they reached the road, Harriet urged the horse to go faster. On and on the sweating horse galloped, all night long.

By morning they had reached a railroad station—a real one, not an underground station— where a Quaker conductor had prepared tickets and passes for the two old people. They would ride in the train's "colored" car, the car for black people, all the way to Wilmington. There Thomas Garrett would meet them.

Harriet went on to Wilmington alone and arrived safely, as she always did. Mr. Garrett had a fresh horse, a buggy, and a driver's uniform waiting for her. With her parents in the buggy and the curtains closed, Harriet drove steadily through Wilmington's crowded streets, disguised as a driver.

At the north edge of town, Harriet whipped the horse into a gallop. The buggy bounced and swayed as they flew down the road toward Pennsylvania. Dogs and chickens jumped out of the way as the horse galloped on. On they went until they had reached the door of the Anti-Slavery Society in Philadelphia. There Harriet let the exhausted horse stop. Old Rit and Daddy Ben were safe for now. Soon they would be on their way to Canada, where they would be truly free.

From 1850 to 1861, Harriet made 19 trips to the South. She led over three hundred slaves to freedom and never lost one. She was never captured. How could this be? The answer was simple, Harriet explained to a friend—she went only where God sent her.

Harriet made her last trip South in 1861, and then she became a scout, nurse, spy, and cook for the Union army during the Civil War. The Emancipation Proclamation of 1863 freed slaves of the southern states as soon as the Union army took those states. Harriet's dream of freedom for her people came true with the passage of the Thirteenth Amendment in 1865, which absolutely outlawed slavery in all parts of the United States.

After the Civil War, Harriet brought her parents back from Canada to live with her in Auburn, New York. In her later years, she continued to devote her life to the needs of others. She spoke out for the rights of women and the newly freed blacks, she cared faithfully for her aged parents, and she opened a home for elderly and needy blacks.

Harriet Tubman died in Auburn in 1913.